Anna Kuusela

The Wander Woman's Playbook –
My Habits for Becoming Unstoppable

Illustrations copyright © 2018 by Nina Pirhonen
Design by Nina Pirhonen
www.ninapirhonen.com

First paperback edition November 2018

ISBN: 9781729363157

Independently Published

To Siiri, Saimi, Elli, and Aarni
Always keep chasing your dreams!

THE 10 HABITS

Dear fellow tribe member,

First of all, thank you for picking up your copy. I'm honoured you're joining me on this journey. A big hug and a warm welcome!

Wow – what an adventure this has been! I've come a long way to make it to where I stand today. It has been hard work, giving up things, winning and losing, tears, and some serious fun. Writing this book has given me a chance to step back, take stock and distill my experiences into a jar of insight I wish I owned 15 years ago.

The idea for the book emerged when I started listening to people around me in a really deep and active way. You see, over the years, I've been approached by handfuls of amazing humans asking me questions of very similar nature, many wearing the same puzzled expressions on their faces. I've witnessed many hopeful souls dreaming large but not sure where to start. These conversations have been invaluable and made me notice something about myself: I had useful insights and valuable things to say, based on the experiences I've gathered.

In May 2018, I found myself in Bali on one of my immersion excursions, learning about the secrets of handstands. Without much thought, I had brought a pile of my old notebooks with me, and while browsing these over my afternoon chai, I realised my excessive (and sometimes obsessive) note-taking, reading, studying, and overall curiosity was presenting me with a tremendous opportunity right in front of me. Before I was aware I had the insight, but now I started thinking I really wanted to share this insight with others! I took my laptop and started to write my thoughts down. I was open to explore where it would lead me...and here I am now, about to publish a book! The process has been cleansing, rejuvenating, and renewing – all at once

I have achieved a lot in my life already, but then again, I was always the big dreamer, keen to set a new standard, so I went after what some perceived impossible. I'm very aware we only have one chance at life, and I wanted to make it count. My professional achievement is my thrilling, decade-long career in management consulting, of which half has been conducted in the wonderful city of London. While to date, I've lived and/or worked in eight countries, learning a tremendous amount, it still feels like yesterday when I arrived in London with no place to live and only about 500 euros in my bank account. In my lifetime, I've had the chance to travel to nearly fifty countries, opening my heart and soul to experiences that have changed me in unimaginable ways. My journey has asked me to gaze into my soul, to interpret the nuts and bolts of who I am, and I like to think I have gone through a personal transformation to become the woman I am today.

I've poured my heart and soul into this book. I've tried to be as transparent and honest as I possibly can, sharing with you my winning moments and the moments I wish to never re-live. These are my lessons learned and things that bring me joy – thoughts and insights I wish I knew when I was a young girl. While I'm aware I have something unique in me, and the amount of passion and dedication I have is enormous, I also have absolute certainty that whatever I've got is available to everyone else as well. What I've done, you can do, too. I don't think I'm special in any way – I have just worked very hard for everything I have today. We all have the gigantic, magical opportunity to achieve our wildest dreams (we only need to know what they are!). I believe it's never too late, and you will never get lost if you follow your heart.

Finally, a few words about habits. What you're about to read are the ten habits that I have designed to support my lifestyle. For me, to form a habit, one needs to have a solid connection between the Why, What and How (Why is the driver, the passion, the ultimate reason; What is the actual what to do; and How is possessing the necessary skills to do it). When this connection exists and a habit becomes a natural part of one's life, there lies a wonderful opportunity for a never-ending upward spiral of personal growth. When we grow and make progress, we are happy. If we don't grow, change and evolve, we will slowly die. I hold each of my habits close to my heart, and I live my life according to them. So, remember, these are my habits, and not all of them will work for everyone. However, I suggest using this as inspiration to live your best life!

Life is a magnificent gift to those who are ready to embrace it. Go after your dreams like you mean it.

With love from Hackney, London

x Anna

ABOUT THE CREATORS

Anna, *the storyteller*

Anna is a small-town girl from Finland. She loves roaming the earth and calls London her current home. She's done a decade-long career in management consulting, advising some of the most talented CEOs of prestigious fashion and luxury houses. Today, Anna wears multiple hats with pride, calling herself a business strategist, coach, author and inspirational speaker. She holds a professional ballet dancer degree, is a yoga enthusiast, an avid reader and an adventure seeker. Her energy is contagious!

Nina, *the illustrator*

Nina is a designer, illustrator and a children's book author from Helsinki, Finland. She and Anna met at a ballet class and both share deep passion for this art form. Nina has great love for prints and strong visuals, which are key elements in both her fashion and textile collections as well as in her illustrations. Curiosity for new ways of working and combining different fields and disciplines gives her inspiration. Find more at ninapirhonen.com or on Instagram @nina_pirhonen. She's a total multi-talent!

WELCOME ON THE ADVENTURE!

First things first, thank you for purchasing my book! I think you're so amazing that I want to give you a gift! How would your own dream-lining plan sound like? Go to my website and download yours – your secret address is:

www.annakuusela.com/youarethebest

Secondly, you're in! A warm welcome to the Wander Woman Tribe! Woop!! The WW Tribe is a next generation tribe for women who make things happen. Behind the tribe lies my personal mission **1+2 by year 2023**.

The 1 stands for 1 million. I am committed to helping 1 million women to live their absolute best lives with high vibration energy, mega confidence and abundance beyond imagination.

The 2 stands for 2 million. I am asking each of these women to return the gift through serving two parties of their choosing. In total this is 2 million women, humans, dogs, organisations, causes... Pay the good stuff forward!

At the heart, the Wander Woman Tribe is not only about showing up for ourselves, it is also about showing up for others. I want to create a space for women who are interested in developing themselves, who love to collaborate and who can see far beyond themselves, understanding and appreciating the fulfilment there lies when we give and contribute to others. You are my tribe!

And, if you're a man – you're welcome, too! Behind every thriving woman is The Man. We love you and we appreciate it requires bravery to stand amongst all these wonderful women. Clearly, you've got what it takes.

So, here's how to hop on the bus...

- Explore more at annakuusela.com or wanderwomantribe.com – a hub for great content, inspiration and an opportunity to get down to business with me. Don't forget to subscribe to my newsletter!
- Stay up to speed with what's going on in nearly real time, either through Instagram @wanderwomantribe, my personal handle @msannaquuu or Facebook @ annawanderwoman. Please use hashtag #wanderwomantribe across all social media platforms so I can see you!
- Send me love letters at anna@annakuusela. com and I will write ya back!

Looking forward to welcoming you to the Tribe!

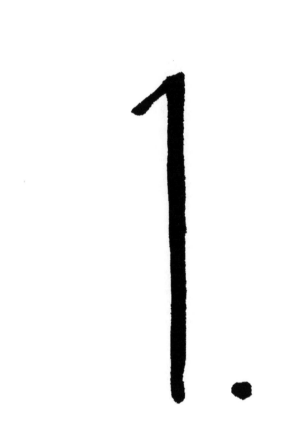

Dream Big

Getting obsessed with my dream

It was a day like any other; however, it was made special by one remarkable idea: to move abroad. This idea made me both ecstatic and terrified at the same time...which made me think this emerging thought needed to be explored further.

I was 27 and living in Helsinki, the capital of Finland. I had a great job at a large consulting house. I was spending time with my passion (dancing ballet) and I was enjoying my newly-found single life, having loads of fun with my girlfriends. My apartment in a hipster neighborhood was gorgeous, and overall, my life was very nice and comfortable. I felt happy, but something was missing.

When I started to look closer, I realised my life didn't look like me. I don't mean it wasn't good, but I felt there was something bigger out there for me. I needed more! I desired to experience more adventures, tap into exciting opportunities, learn about life, feel alive, laugh until it hurts, travel, speak foreign languages, get lost, fall in love, and see the world. I was quick to admit to myself that I was bored with my current situation. Everything in my life was so comfortable that for a person whose primary values were uncertainty and variety, I was going nowhere.

The other thing that had started to bother me back then was the prescribed lives we all are assumed to embrace and get on with, no questions asked. I'm talking about the journey of "education, job, marriage, mortgage, kids." To me, it felt foreign, but in real life, no other concepts seemed to exist. I held the belief that we can do whatever we want in our lives, and I wanted to do things my way, but I wasn't sure yet what "my way" was. The rebel side of me was having the time of her life.

I cannot deny how excited the whole idea of moving abroad made me! (Sure, it was accompanied by a tiny voice somewhere inside my head telling me I must be crazy. It made me uneasy, but I recognised it as a limiting belief I needed to break. To do this I started conditioning myself saying over and over again, "*I can do this*".) When the secretive darkness of the night arrived and I closed my eyes, all my five senses went to work, creating such exquisite visions of my future, it felt like I was living there. I could almost touch it. Waking up, I felt my soul was on fire, and I could feel the force pushing me to do something about my dream.

To make a decision is often the hardest part in anything. I knew it, so I made my decision very swiftly to avoid backing up. I was going to move to London! I knew this dream would unlock many good, bad, and ugly things in both myself and my life, and I was ready to embrace all of it.

Now is always the best time

*B*e careful what you wish for because you might get it... That is exactly what happened to me! After getting the seemingly innocent idea of moving into my head, I now suddenly live in London and have realised dreams that at first seemed impossible. How did this happen? I worked for it. Was it worth the risk? For sure. Would I do it again? In a heartbeat.

I never adored the "*when then*" lifestyle (you know, *when* I have this, *then* I will...) and perhaps as a rebellious act towards this, I developed a mindset of *now is always the best time* and decided there was no such thing as a perfect moment. I think we are never ready, and if we wait until we are ready, we will be waiting for the rest of our lives. Personally, I had no time to waste – I had a huge hunger to get on with my life. This mindset was a significant driving force behind my life-altering decision.

When I look back now, I can see I got quite a few things right, considering this was the first time I was doing a relocation of this magnitude. First of all, I was lucky in a sense that I was over the moon about my dream: this made me ecstatic and kept me pursuing my goal, even when it seemed like there was a never-ending queue of challenges ahead of me – think finding work, flat, friends...some big stuff. The other thing was my brutal honesty about the gap between my idea and an executable plan. This gap was the size of the Amazon rainforest. Yes, some work would be required here.

That "*some work*" ended up being I'm-going-to-faint-if-there's-even-one-more-task amount of work. I prefer executing on a plan, not an idea, so I called the left-hand side of my brain to work. But, to know where to start is a challenge in itself!

The task seemed hairy, scary and audacious. In addition, I personally don't deal well with abstract things, and I'm a very simple person, so I decided to take it to another level and did what I do best: making lists, organising, and chunking things into categories.

I wrote down absolutely everything that was bothering me about the move, from paying taxes to the neighbourhood I should live in – things I thought I ought to know. I Googled from A to Z, and I reached out to people who were living in London, who had lived in London, or who knew someone who lives in London. I didn't care. I wanted to know it all. I read a million miles of webpages, white papers, conversations and chats. I wrote everything down. Call it obsession but I wanted to be prepared for whatever London would throw at me.

I didn't ignore my home terrain either. I quit my job (woah!), rented the flat and sold my stuff – the money certainly warmed my pockets. I did a regular strategy meeting with myself and got very realistic about where I stood in comparison to London, one of the most competitive, creative and hard-working cities in the world. I looked into my skillset, but more than that, I looked into my mental strength: I believe it's 80% psychology and the rest is tools and techniques. Throughout the process, I kept telling myself, *"What if this was easy?"*. I wanted to make it feel easy, but more importantly, I knew I needed to have some serious mental stamina to make it in London.

Finally, I felt (somewhat) ready to step away from my comfort zone in a big way. In about nine months from planting the idea of moving, I was holding my one-way ticket to London in my hand. I could feel a grand adventure was about to start.

To anyone who wants to get dreamy now, I'd love to say...

- We humans have this extraordinary capability to dream – so dream! The more real and vivid they are, the better chance there is to make them come true. Where you focus, your energy follows...and the universe gives!

- Be so obsessed about the dream you're ready to hustle for it! Don't wait but start to act today. Today! Keep reminding yourself of the dream so your beliefs, thoughts and actions start to align. Have a vision board next to your bed you can look at each morning and night.

- Believe, believe, believe. You start to see opportunities in the most unexpected places.

2.

Live in a Strong Body

Everything starts with movement

I did my first dance class when I was 5 years old – little did I know this class would mark the start of a lifetime journey with movement. Dancing (while holding pink scarves in my hands and floating through the room like a feather) made me feel like I had arrived somewhere familiar. It opened the door for me to explore the world and myself through my physical body. Dancing allows my true nature to come out, and it lets me have some serious fun. I continue to be amazed with what my body is capable of. I often say that I go to my dance class with problems and leave with solutions.

Certainly, my dance journey has had its rigorous elements, too. I started my formal 10-year classical ballet training at the age of eight, and I rehearsed tens of thousands of hours not to only perfect my plié, développé and adage, but to learn about the history of dance, anatomy, different styles of movement and about becoming a performance artist. It's hard to try to distil this part of me into words but what I can say with certainty is that dance – and movement overall – is a huge part of my identity.

Adding London to the above picture made me re-think my approach to movement. It can get quite brutal when it comes to work/life balance in this town. To be completely honest, I'm not sure there is such thing as *balance*. After the honeymoon period with London was over and I started experiencing first-hand what *fast-paced* can mean in all its glory, some of my thinking shifted like tectonic plates. I am sure 80-hour work weeks, sitting in the worst chairs in the smallest cupboards with little or no time for lunch, with the added bonus of having constant pressure about delivering high-quality work, would most likely make everyone else ponder the same profound questions I did.

At the same time, my lower back started to act up. I had a hard time sitting at my desk for even one whole hour! I went to see a doctor, and after the MRI scan, the opinion of three different specialists was more or less the same: my back needed to be operated on and I would never dance ballet again. High heels were out of the picture, too. My world fell apart. How could this happen? I get ballet is tough on the body, but I wasn't even 30 years old.

I was not going to accept the diagnosis. I thought, there must be another way. I also understood my health was not to be taken for granted anymore, but I needed to do something to maintain and improve my wellbeing. I started a rigorous search for professionals who could help me. I needed someone who could understand a ballet/consultant body (aka a very messed up physique) and who would give me the permission to continue dancing. Ask and you shall receive! In a few weeks, I got a phone number for a physio who, according to my dancer friends, was like a miracle worker. And boy, did she live up to these words. All she needed was a ten-second scan up and down my body and I heard her saying, "Anna, you have a bio-mechanical issue in your lower body, and we can fix this in very little time. No surgery required." I cried all the way back home.

After being stopped in my tracks, my approach to movement changed considerably. I could no longer move just for fun, but it was required to keep me mobile. I decided to update my lifestyle once and for all. I kept doing my yoga practice and going to my dance classes as per my usual style, but on top of that, I started making conscious choices to eat clean and vegetarian, to drink plenty of water and to get a regular seven hours of sleep each and every night. (To be honest, the sleeping part has been the hardest piece in the puzzle – why is there only 24 hours a day?!) Anyhow, I also added movement into my work life: taking the stairs, doing the happy dance, not sitting for too long – whatever was required to keep my body moving throughout the day. I also changed my approach to rest, accepting there are days when I do not have to move. I started to listen to what my body was telling me.

All this made a huge impact on my overall wellbeing. The increase in daily movement, even if it was only a tiny positive change in my physiology, increased my energy levels, and when my energy was higher, I was able to do and achieve more. I was liking it! I started to understand how much wisdom there is in my body and that my body really is the source for my wellbeing, energy, vitality and life. Today, I know that when I live in a strong body, I can maximise my potential in life.

Priming myself for life

I'm such a morning bird. I've always loved waking up before the rest of the world. By the time most people get to their daily duties, I have already done things I love and enjoy.

It was a few years ago when I started buying into the concept of *we are what we do daily.* I happened to have a very detailed picture of the woman I wanted to be. However, between that woman and today, there was a gap. I didn't need to ask Sherlock Holmes for help to realise my work was making this gap bigger by the day. I was working way too many hours and being reactive with...well, everything. I knew to take back control and to breathe more energy into my life, something would need to change.

Being the smart lady I am, I put one and one together and understood mornings can help me increase the quality of my life because I could spend time on doing things I really care about. I started exploring different ways to make my mornings matter – and I was not the first to study this in more detail! The amount of research, books and YouTube tutorials on the topic is mind-numbing! They helped me to grasp mornings are my opportunity to focus on the most important asset of my world: myself. Through moving my body, meditation and breathwork, water and food, I can elevate my state and make my mind laser-focused for the day ahead. My morning routine sets me up for the day, makes me feel good about myself, and leaves me energised. Where I focus, my energy will follow, and this is what my morning priming is all about.

I can easily spend three hours on my morning stuff, but if I have five minutes, I'll take it. The following structure is currently my ideal way to spend my morning:

- I wake up early enough so I don't need to rush – I dislike getting my blood pressure high first thing in the morning. I try to drink as much water as I can in the next few hours and start moving my body – typically, I either run, cycle or do yoga. I don't really think about anything much before I've done my dose of movement. After this, I'm in a better state and can think straight.

- Then I concentrate on my breathing and meditation exercises, and this can be anything from 10 to 30 minutes. My breathing exercises and visualisation have been powerful to me, helping me raise my awareness to things I might not otherwise pay any attention to and getting crystal clear on my goals. I am also a fan of gratefulness practice in the morning to set the mood right. I notice the busier my life gets and the more people I meet and try to help, the more I need this time. It lets me restore my own energy.

- After exercise, I jump into a cold shower – there's nothing like freezing cold water waking up the last dormant cells in my body. The colder the better. I hate it first, but I know I'll love it later. If there's an option to run into the sea, even better.

- Now I am ready to write. I plan my life, months, weeks and days. If it's not in my diary, it's not going to happen! I spend time reviewing what I need to achieve on that day and make sure I'm in the right state to do all my actions.

- Finally, I don't leave the house hungry: I focus on greens in the morning in order to alkalise the body, and I keep drinking that water.

My morning routine is single-handedly one of the most important factors in my life. These days, when I leave home in the morning, I don't care if there's Santa Claus and his reindeer falling from the sky – I'm ready to take on all the opportunities the world offers, and other people's bad weather won't take me down. Win the morning, win the day!

3.

Ooze Confidence and Be Yourself

My confidence-muscle

I'm often told, *"Oh, but that's so easy for you because you're confident."* And that is true – I am confident because I have taught myself to be confident! If I don't believe I'm worthy, who will?!

At the start of elementary school, I was a small, white-haired girl with huge red glasses, a gap between my front teeth, a very loud voice, and perhaps a bit too eager to share my opinions. A few years later, you could see me sporting a pair of bright yellow jeans matched with a lime green satin shirt (yes, you read that right). While this was certainly a fabulous outfit, for me, it was also an opportunity to express my unique being. Even back then, I could already feel *that something* within me that wanted to come out, and I was keen to explore it, be it through my clothes, my communication or just my being. I didn't really care what others would say – and believe me, I have gotten my fair share of bullying and nasty comments – but I kept thinking, *I'm heading somewhere and good things will come out of this.* Deep inside, I thought others' opinions had nothing to do with me – and I kept wearing those fab yellow jeans.

So, I kept going, unknowingly working on my confidence-mindset. I thought if my head was strong enough, it wouldn't get hurt by minor comments or other people's opinions about me. I realised my validation needed to come from my very core and not from external sources. To strengthen this, I told myself empowering stories and kept seeing myself in a positive light. This translated to other parts of my life. For example, in ballet, which is a very disciplined art form, I approached the daily grind with determination, keen to systematically improve myself each and every day. I had a clear goal and I was in competition with myself, not anyone else.

Today, I can easily see the psychological importance of training this mindset throughout my adolescence, and I think my idea to love and trust myself first has been one of the foundational building blocks of the strong character I possess today. Add the support from my parents who always wanted me to succeed in whatever it was I wanted to do with my life, my foundation is rock solid.

Since I have been working on my confidence for a proper while, a positive and empowered state now comes to me relatively automatically these days. When I need some pumping up (and I still sometimes do!), there are a few techniques I have established that I can fully rely on. I know many of these will feel very strange in the beginning, but I'm a living proof that it will all come together after practice, practice, practice...

- Capability gives confidence. I know my stuff – and if I don't know it, I will learn it.

- Visualisation of what sort of woman I want to be and then being that woman! I visualise how she would behave, act, talk, listen, and be in different situations. Fake it 'till you make it!

- Telling myself I am worthy and capable – and this needs to happen out and aloud: *I can do this! I'm a gladiator!* Repeat. Repeat. Repeat! I have created several music playlists to support different states and moods...there's nothing quite like blasting the song '*Uprising*' by Muse first thing on Monday morning!

- Power posing for a Wander Woman effect. Priming my body to ensure that I use my body language efficiently, for example, when entering and taking space. This has a huge positive impact on the brain.

- Getting my image right: How I shake hands with people, introduce myself and what I wear. First impressions can only be made once. I never underestimate the importance of how things (or I) look; so I dress, speak and act according to the occasion.

- Focusing on getting the message and language right: Ensuring my words and language fit the context. Overall, I don't like too many softeners and prefer to maintain my no-nonsense, practical (and Finnish) approach.

Finally, I should say my ideal woman is a moving target (hence I keep working on my confidence muscle), however I know my building blocks are solid and I can represent myself in an authentic way in all situations. This is a good foundation to build on.

Being different (...or a woman)

" *We would be so pleased to have you in this pitch as an expert on digital in retail.*"

I was blushing. Yes, they wanted me! The consulting partner called me an expert! I must be amazing! The next day, I received the pitch presentation card for review. After a quick browse, I thought the content seemed on point, my photo was decent (very important, obvs), and the whole pitch team was looking strong, suited, and booted...Michael, Joe, Dan, George, Thomas, Henry.... Can you see where I'm going here? Yep, I was the diversity card! They wanted me in the pitch because I'm a woman.

This is not the first time this has happened – and it will certainly not be the last. While I've been truly privileged to work with some amazing colleagues and clients, it's not fun and games at all times. In my line of work, there's not that many women, and it has become more male-dominated as I have climbed up the ladder. This has been one of the funniest conundrums for me to work out: the *good* thing is, people will usually remember me because

I'm the only woman. The *bad* thing is, people will often remember me because I'm the only woman. Anyhow...I have had my time with clients who have had an issue with me being a woman. I've had colleagues who have dismissed me clearly due to my gender. In some instances, I have been required to work harder than others (dare I say men?!) to be given the permission to play.

Did I complain? Nope. Did I step back so that others could lean in? Absolutely not. Did I go to this pitch I mentioned above, work harder than ever to ensure I'd be amazing, AND wear my pink suit, nailing it all?! Abso-effing-lutely!

The question for me is, what do I make out of all of this? First of all, I have always been proud to be a woman. Every time I have the chance to benefit from my gender, I will shamelessly do it. I will never apologise for being a woman – even better, I will never apologise for being a *confident* woman. Secondly, all of us, women or men, need to believe we are enough the way we are now. The fear of not being loved or not being enough is real for many, and it easily translates into a handicapping belief, even at work. Finally, we have the choice to address a meaning to everything: I will decide what I hear from my environment and the impact I will let that have on me. I will not be defeated by those who keep chucking their expensive opinions from cheap seats – those opinions do not improve my life at all, so I choose to ignore them. Remember, others' opinions about you are none of your business.

If I have learned something from my consulting career, it is the importance of the right environment. We need to remember we cannot change others; we can only change ourselves. When I have felt the most at home and achieved some major wins in my career, I have always been in the right environment, supported by an amazing team of bosses and colleagues. They have been more interested in what I can do today and in helping me to improve for tomorrow rather than making my gender a focal point. This is what I call a true win-win situation. When my leadership team has been diverse in their gender and thinking, it has set a good tone for the underpinning organisation culture, unlocking a thriving business and happy team.

The future is both female and male as I see it. It is crucial how men step up and support us women, but it is even more important how us women support other women – including peers, bosses and junior members of the team. We need to be creating rules that enable us to win. We need to empower other women at all levels to be the leaders of today and tomorrow. We are required to embrace what we can do, what unique things we bring to the table, what valuable insights we have – not what gender we represent. Together, we are so powerful and all of us have a lot to give – women included.

4.

Know What You Want and Put in The Work

Knowing what I want

When I was writing the final chapters of my master's thesis, an unsettling emotion started to surface. I recognised I was clueless about what I wanted to do with my life after I graduated! To add to my panic, it seemed like everyone else had their life together and I was a hot mess.

After tearing half my hair out, I understood I needed to get laser-focused to pin this baby down. I tried to see to the end of the rainbow, and I thought I saw some flying unicorns there. Indeed, the world is open once you shut those university doors: I could go in whatever direction I wanted...so, I went to my ballet class. After sweating for 90 minutes, I got home and wrote my wildest career objectives in my notebook. This was it. I had a place to start.

It was a beautiful mid-week fall day when I returned my thesis. The next day, on the first day of the rest of my life, I was determined to find a job that would match my criteria. Opening my laptop and browsing for jobs, I could see there were a few management consultant positions open. I had always had a slightly negative opinion about this profession if I'm honest, mainly because I thought it's not actually a proper job. However, now I saw myself looking into the details of this role (hey, I really was in need of a job...). Suddenly, I started to see how this job was ticking quite a few of my career objective boxes. Hold on a moment...should I apply to a job I never thought I would be interested in?!

Before you can say *alavilla mailla hallan vaara* (some beautiful Finnish for you there!), I had applied for the position and was diving head-first into a three-round consulting interview washing machine. I remember being so nervous I couldn't eat. I definitely wasn't functioning like a normal human being. On the first round of interviews, I met a bunch of other candidates, and oh boy, these guys were smart! They were speaking a language I had never heard of (lean six sigma, operating models, CRM...come on!). It made me very curious. What was this job so many people wanted? Who were all these people? What could I learn from them?

It was clear I was the underdog – but also, I had nothing to lose. So, I decided to show up with everything I had. In my cheap (but well-ironed) suit,

I approached the entire process with determination and a willingness to learn. I got through round after round and finally, when I was due to interview with the head honcho (the partner), I was in an ecstatic state. I was young, I was hungry – but more than that, I wanted this job. I wanted this job to be mine so badly.

Did I think I was ready? No! Was I confident I could actually do this job? Absolutely not! Did I believe this opportunity belonged to me and was I willing to step up and show them the passion I was going to bring in to the table? 110% YES!

In a heartbeat, it was all over and a long period of silence started. I'm still terrible at waiting; I have no patience whatsoever. Then, a day before Christmas Eve, my phone rang, and it was the very same head honcho. I nearly collapsed when I heard him say, *"Anna, we had over two hundred applicants, and we have decided to make two offers, and I'm making the other one to you now."* Obviously, I said, *"Yes, I'll take it! Thank you very much!"*

It was me who made the outcome happen. I showed up and did the work. I deserved this job. I was one happy junior management consultant.

Working like a boss

As I have stated I don't think I possess any superwoman abilities, however I can honestly say I've been slaying like a boss since my kindergarten days. Looking from the outside, I was the weird tall one with poor external rotation in ballet and I definitely wasn't any Einstein at school. However, I had passion for life, I was hungry to learn, and I never, ever wanted to give up.

Now, a few years later (!), I definitely haven't arrived to where I am today by chance – nor was it all by design, but what I know for sure is that I have spent a considerable amount of time articulating my goals in life and putting in countless hours of dedicated and determined work to make sure I do everything that is in my power to reach these goals. Let me quickly dwell on my career to give you an idea of what putting in the work means here...

Indeed, looking at what I've accomplished in my career to date, I want to give myself a pat on the back. During my decade-long management consulting career, I've done everything from strategy to implementation, working with various industries from construction companies to fast fashion businesses. Time has flown by as I have represented both large corporations and smaller boutique consultancies. I've progressed swiftly from an analyst fixing spreadsheets into a trusted advisor helping CEOs with their most challenging topics. The nature of this particular profession has ignited my passion, constantly leaving me hungry for more, and I can easily say consulting has fit my personality really well, catering for the left and right sides of my brain and allowing me to create a positive impact in my clients' businesses.

A little nudge from the universe won't hurt either – arriving to the UK six years ago was somewhat of a perfect storm. Technology and globalisation were still changing the game and suddenly, the relatively traditional consulting industry was required to solve new types of client problems, asking consultants to quickly come up with new tools and fresh ideas. I seemed to possess many advantages and found my team who gave me the opportunity to stand in the eye of this storm. I was privileged to join a company whose vision was to create value in client organisations in a way I had never seen before, and all the work was underpinned by an exceptional organisational culture.

For five years, as part of this family, I focused on leading and delivering complex organisational change with my team and client CEOs, accompanied by their leadership teams. What made it extra hard was that I was not only responsible for the design of things, but I also needed to execute on them – I can tell you it's an entirely different game when you need to practice what you preach...! I focused on fashion and luxury businesses and became a specialist in customer experience, business models, operating models and change management. For many, this might sound like Latin, so basically, I was in charge of the design of a company's engine, and I helped the client to reach their vision through improving the nuts and bolts of that engine. So, really, I'm very good at fixing other people's problems – and businesses.

I've made my mistakes during these years, trying to understand how I work the best and how to reach the best outcome for everyone. I still have moments when I don't have a clue what I'm doing. But what I do know is how to work the most efficiently. Here are some of my principles I've gathered throughout my consulting career:

- Practice, practice, practice. It requires 10,000 repetitions to master a skill. From my ballet background, I can easily see how this can be true. Even today, when I go to a ballet class, we repeat the simplest of steps. The work never ends!

- I practice deeply with any new skill, like standing on my hands. When I feel it's not going to work in a million years, I start to be close to a breakthrough. I do one more, I try once more, just one more...letting the poor brain cells operate on the edge. This is where improvement happens.

- Understanding what my preferred modus operandi is. I am a morning person and do my best work in the early morning hours. If I need to do deep work, an open office is not the best place for me. I get my best ideas when I'm moving my body or talking with my colleagues.

- Batching work. Not all work is created equal. I batch work in order to be more efficient. For example, I focus on replying to all of the emails in a one-hour afternoon slot, and

Mondays are my days to get admin tasks sorted. This approach will save time.

- I plan everything. I don't execute on an idea but on a plan. If something is not in my diary, it's not going to happen. Time is our most precious asset, and we will never get it back. I'm the master of my diary.

- Ideally, I avoid multitasking. Our brains were not designed to do a million things at once, so don't. I try to focus on the matter at hand and get it done and dusted. I have to admit, I'm still not very good at this.

- I take regular breaks and make sure I move my body throughout the day.

To say the least, my work has been super exciting! I always say what I've learned in London in these six years might have taken me quite a lot longer back home in Finland, so quick is the pace. My love for thinking outside the box, making complex things simple, finding pockets of value and connecting dots across the unimagined were on fire as I kept powering through some very long weeks, a lot of travel and challenging client engagements. I never wanted to chill. I thought, if I do that, someone else is working and winning it.

(Psst! If you want to learn more, there are some tips for working in management consulting at the end of the book!)

Learning more and expanding myself

As a kid, going to the library was the highlight of my week. I could spend considerable time between the tall book shelves, selecting titles I heard were whispering my name. I remember having the same conversation with my mom each time: "*Anna, are you really going to borrow that huge pile and read it, too?*" I was adamant, and somehow, I always got through the mountain of books. I wanted to know everything about everything, and books opened up a new universe where fascinating adventures were presented to those who dared.

We humans are curious by nature, and when we feed this curiosity, we become more of everything.

As I said, I have never thought I'm naturally talented; therefore, I was always open to explore how I could improve. Reflecting back, I can see how all my best intentions to learn and to experience have made me this delightfully complex woman I am today. This complexity is to be desired, for it makes us extraordinary and sets us apart from robots, computers and all things artificial. Through fine-tuning (and sometimes completely transforming) our bodies, spirits and our brains (still the best computer of them all, by the way), we have the opportunity to thrive and achieve what we were set out to do.

Learning is an attitude towards life. This attitude has made me open minded and flexible, which in turn has made me less fearful. When I behave this way, it is almost like I can perceive more opportunities around me. In addition, I don't work to earn; I work to learn. This mindset has considerably improved my life, the quality of my interactions and the outcomes of my work. It also makes life more fun! Distilling the above into a list could look something like this...

- Consume quality content. Garbage in is garbage out

- Learn from the best and you'll learn much quicker and have a better chance to make it right the first time around. Success leaves clues so look for people who've done it before.

- Invest time and some serious dinero. When you're more committed, you work harder and – surprise – get better results.

- Make it fun. Kids learn quickly because they make it fun. Have fun hobbies!

- Leaders read! Dedicating 20-30 minutes per day makes a big difference in a year.

- Be willing to sacrifice things. Watching TV takes you nowhere. Make conscious decisions about how you spend your free time.

- Ask good questions – from yourself and others. Quality questions give you quality answers.

- Don't lose your curiosity when you grow up. Even better, never grow up. ☺

When we focus on building our toolbox through catering our passions, we make ourselves unique through our skills and attitudes. This furthermore positions us to win in the marketplace, whatever the conditions are. I keep reminding myself that if I don't challenge myself, it will slowly make me complacent and boring, with nothing interesting to say.

5.

Be a Leader

Leading myself before I lead others

I have always been interested in leadership. Even as a young girl, I happily took on opportunities that to some, might look like leading: chairing a board, leading a team of cheerleaders (I know!) or performing a leading role in a ballet. However, I never thought I was *the leader*; I just wanted to step up, take more responsibility, and achieve more through trying new things while showing the world what I can do.

Later on, consulting gave me a crash course in leadership. To do well in this profession, some emotional self-mastery is necessary. Consulting projects can get very stressful. They are always time-constrained, and the quality of the work is regularly challenged. It would be easier to reactively pin-ball from one emotion to another rather than to control them (and my own stress levels) mindfully and consciously. In addition, the type of work I have undertaken includes a lot of change to which individuals respond differently. I need to manage myself and my energy levels while not getting too emotional, as too many emotions in the game will make my client more confused and blur the goal.

Knowing my *"operating system"* has been crucial to developing my leadership skills. (By the way, I believe leadership is a skillset anyone can learn. Leadership has nothing to do with age, job, or rank, but it's more about the right mindset.) Understanding my core values, beliefs and rules in detail and therefore gaining more control over my own psychology is vital to leading a good life, never mind leading others to a good life! When I can control my psychology and emotions, it gives me superpowers – and from consulting, I know that when I bring my best energy and emotions into the game, things start to happen.

When I think about people I admire – from Barack Obama to Yves Saint Laurent and from Misty Copeland to Yuval Noah Harari – I realise they possess similar characteristics. They act with utmost integrity, elegance and poise, and there's almost something alluring in them that makes me want to follow them...and I would not mind them leading me!

Reflecting back on this now, this is how I started leading myself...

- I read a huge pile of self-help books (see my list in the back!), working on the 'inner me' – my beliefs, thoughts, actions and habits. Ultimately, what we believe becomes our life.

- I started observing how I talk to myself. You wouldn't tell your friend she's terrible so why do you keep telling that to yourself?

- I kept an eye on the language that comes out of my mouth as well. My thought is to stay silent more and use my words wisely. Words strengthen our beliefs and send out a message to the world what we really stand up for. Don't stand up for s***.

- I looked for opportunities to lead – they are plentiful because so many people are afraid to step up. Don't be that person, the world needs leaders.

Being a leader wherever I am

I was at the bottom of my bed, suffering from the flu of a lifetime. Classic over-achiever symptom, being unwell while on holiday! However, this nasty bug was showing no signs of leaving my body and when it was time to go back to my desk I was still feeling weak. My boss was on holiday, and I merrily told him not to worry; I could easily manage my team from my bed turned office with the help of my mobile phone.

After another week, I returned to work to find out my team had made progress in the project – the only problem was they had made progress in the wrong direction. I wanted to faint when I thought about the enormous pile of work I would personally need to do to fix it all. My team happily pottered on and seemed to be clueless as to what was going on.

It was time for our morning meeting, and I had carefully crafted my instructions to the team on what we would need to do this week. (The task was basically to change everything they had accomplished last week. Hmm, I know...) I was pretty sure this was not going to go down well. However

I was surprised to find out my team was almost as surprised as I was – they looked like they had no idea the quality and content of the work was not meeting expectations at all. I could sense the team was irritated with me, and they looked like they would be more interested in reading the newspaper in Chinese rather than continuing working for me. However, I kept my cool and re-iterated the changes that would need to take place. Leaving the meeting, the atmosphere resembled a freezing winter day in Finland, only colder.

As I lost my ability to influence my team, I painfully learned the key skill of leadership: influencing others. At the heart of any good leadership is to understand where others are coming from and how best to interact with them in order to reach any goal. We need to have the desire to step into their shoes with the greatest of empathy. Yeah, that was not me back in the days. While my team was coming from a good place, they were blindfolded by my unclear instructions. Terrible leadership. Why do the life lessons sometimes need to be this painful?!

Well, I took my own medicine, returned back home to my bed and spent a long night thinking about what sort of leader I wanted to be. I listed all my teachers and leaders I had been inspired by and wrote down what had made them so remarkable. Here are some of those bullet points:

- They have their own style. They are very authentic and comfortable with who they are. I have had quiet bosses, very charismatic ones, intellectual geeks and some crazy extroverts, and I love them all!

- They never judge

- They make good decisions at pace

- They are mature in all of their communications and exceptionally talented at listening to me and understanding my unique situation

- They walk their talk and are consistent at all times – from how they behave to what they say and the clothes they wear. However, they can change their opinion in a blink of an eye if they see there's a good reason for it.

- They know where we are going and are able to get people on the same bus. They don't mind if I craft my own way, even when it looks different to what they had in mind.

- They see when I'm tired and ask how they can help.

- They recognise when I've been working hard and give praise.

- They help me to understand my own strengths and weaknesses, supporting my growth journey.

- Finally, they have something special about them, something that makes it really difficult to say no to them!

6.

Pursue Joyfulness and Have Fun

My life is an adventure...yours?

My life is an adventure, and I'm planning to have a lot of fun while I'm at it! I don't think anyone ever said, *I wish I had less fun.* I always wish I had more!

My goal is to have fun each and every day. We are what we do daily! My simple recipe is to keep doing things that bring me joy. I have a list of 30 or so odd things that I know will instantly make me feel good, joyful and almost ecstatic! These are things that are in my control zone, don't necessarily cost a dime and will certainly elevate my state. Having this positive state in my life is vital: it creates more energy, makes me more resourceful and therefore increases my chances to be successful, whatever it is I'm up to. I have also experienced that when I'm having a good time, the universe loves me more and things work *for* me, not *against* me.

So, day in, day out, I move my body (#1 on my *Be Happy* list), listen to music (#2), Skype with my nieces (#3), journal (#6), call my mom (#9), burn scented candles (#11), organise my desk (weird, I know...,

#13), or take a nap (#27). However, I have also done a bungee jump, leaped from a 30ft pole and walked on fire. Why? Because I believe every now and then we need to go beyond our comfort zones and do things that are in the experience level 10+! This will make our lives richer, we might (secretly) enjoy it and after this, the "normal" stuff is fun again!

What has definitely made me better at having fun and enjoying life is how I have made my "rules" work for me. Rules are our beliefs about what needs to happen in order for us to feel good about a certain experience. If the rules are very strict and inflexible, it is harder to be happy. My favourite rule that works like magic each and every time is that going to my dance class will make me happier. No other expectations. If I said going to my dance class *and* doing a triple pirouette ending in splits jump up in the air is a prerequisite for happiness, I think I'd be less happy... ☺ This is about setting a high standard for yourself and living your life according to your own (high) standards with the right dose of flexibility!

To create lasting joy and happiness in life requires the skill to get fully immersed with the present moment, enjoying what we have now. Thi requires practice – us humans always want more and it's always easier to complain and be negative rather than to find appreciation in the present state. I don't wait to have fun when I'm slimmer/on holiday/finish the exams, as I know I'll be feeling exactly the same as I did prior to the experience, and this in turn is disappointing. The best time to have fun is now, but the brain needs to be conditioned for it.

My simple recipe to have more fun in life:

- I practice gratitude – being grateful what I have now is a starting point for getting more of any good stuff. Really, ANY good stuff.

- I go back to my *Be Happy* list as often as I need to – sometimes this might be a few times in a hot minute when I've completely lost my mojo.

- I'm not afraid of looking like a weirdo when I have fun – best case scenario I might even be making someone else's day!

- This is embarrassing but I'll say it anyways: I'll put the fun in my diary so I'll remember to have it ☺

- I reward myself when things go according to plan. This can be anything from a small victory dance to a weekend in Paris. It's paramount to create moments of celebration.

The final disclaimer is that life is not always fun, and that's ok. It is not supposed to be. We face ups and downs, and all emotions are beautiful. However, we can live in whatever emotion we desire, and changing an emotion to another in a heartbeat is an acquired skill. Moreover, it's also an attitude. When life gives us lemons (and it will!), do we say thank you and grow or do we get upset? This is a choice each one of us can make.

予.

Keep Practising Life

Not knowing it all

I faced many challenges when settling in London: finding a flat to call home while ensuring the flatmates were somewhat normal citizens; being interviewed for a national insurance number while a drunken person shouted in the lobby; researching jobs, calling headhunters, and running from one interview to another across London in high heels; going to the bank about three times to get a bank account opened; not finding any of the Finnish food staples in the neighbourhood Tesco. I still have a hard time believing it, but it was easier and quicker to get a job than opening a bank account... go figure!

The interesting thing about moving abroad is that I started looking at the banalest, daily things with new eyes. Suddenly, the traffic was on the left. Planning commute was a daily activity, and I had no idea what people were talking about when it came to TV. And yes, it was a struggle to deal with things in a foreign language *all day long.* This phase took a while, but the good thing is, once it was done, it was done.

While I was expecting some of the above, it was the rush of loneliness that hit me hard. I had not prepared for it. It's almost funny, having ten million people around me and no one to talk to! I'm as extroverted as one can get, but moving as an adult made me feel like the new kid on the block: a bit awkward, shy and intimidated. By adulthood, most of us have developed firm circles of friendships around us, so fitting in can be a struggle.

That said, there were people out there who were on the same journey; I just needed to take the driver's seat, go out, meet people and start talking to them! When I approached others with authenticity, an open mind, and showing genuine interest in each and every individual and their life stories, I received the warmest response. I found new friends in many places: in my yoga studio, at my dance class, in coffee shops, at a housemate's party. It took some time for sure, but it made London feel so much more like home.

Also, let me just point out that moving abroad is a journey of a lifetime! While all of the above can be seen as massive hurdles, the sense of adventure gave me a lot of energy to tackle many of these challenges. In addition, my realisation to accept myself as a beginner was a game-changer: I'm talking about not knowing if all, asking others for help, leaning into others for their insight. I didn't take any of this as a sign of weakness; instead, it meant I was being proactive and positive with a doer attitude, and this definitely helped me to adapt and settle in to my new environment swiftly.

Finally, once the building blocks were in place, the feeling of joy was of a magnitude that made me feel very happy. I had done all this by myself – I felt stronger, more capable, and I knew that whatever life would throw at me in the future, I would be able to handle it.

Loving language barriers

"*Anna, you know what—when you talk, people get curious instantly because you sound different. You are a foreigner with a beautiful accent!*"

This is what one of my former colleagues, an English gentleman, told me, and it completely changed my perspective. Before that, I had been afraid of making multiple mistakes and sounding funny, but now, my accent had suddenly become my asset!

The thing is, coming from Finland, it's not like I started speaking English yesterday. Most Finns do speak English; they just need some time to gather their courage (and to make sure whatever comes out of their mouths is 100% correct). I myself went to an English kindergarten at the age of five and clearly pronounced the word s*** at age six (accidentally, obvs). My mouth was washed with soap right there! So, you could say I knew what I was doing (or should I say speaking) when I moved to London.

There's another thing about us Finns you ought to know... In our language, we don't have a separate word for *please*. Yes, you read that right. This means that the Finnish language is constructed quite uniquely, and even though we have polite ways of articulating ourselves in Finnish, we tend to come across too directly for native English speakers, Brits in particular. My approach has been to stick *please* everywhere and hope for the best. To my own surprise, my experience over the years has been that when people get to know me, they start to value the *Finnish way* of communication (aka being the most direct person in the room). One of my clients even once told me how she liked that I actually say what I mean!

That said, once I immersed myself fully into the British culture, I learned its deep-rooted cultural customs. One of the most obvious ones is the dislike of silence. Us Finns love silence – and this further translates into the lack of small talk. While Brits get uncomfortable quickly if there are breaks in communication, Finns can continue being silent, barely nodding our heads and agreeing with everything we hear. I needed to practice my small talk skills in order to fit in better...and I can say, there's a lot of talking just for the sake of it! During my first London year, I remember getting home from work and wanting to be silent for the rest of the evening. My brain was on double duty, translating things from English to Finnish and vice versa while repeating *please* at regular intervals. While today, I'm very comfortable with my professional English, I am embarrassed to admit I continue to struggle with the alphabet: the English "I" is the Finnish "A"; the English "E" is the Finnish "I"; "A" is the Finnish "E"...confused already? I still am!

In the end, I'm fortunate to be able to express myself in five different languages – heck I've written this book in English! (Yes, I'm sure there are mistakes, but nevertheless...) Speaking different languages is a true gift, allowing me to engage with foreign people and their cultures on a completely new level. It has also made my personality richer. I think I'm funnier in Finnish. The English version of me can be very poised. I cannot talk about my work in Finnish that well. I'm better equipped at voicing some of my emotions in Finnish (we have about 60 words for snow alone!). I am proud of my accent, I am ok to make mistakes, and I am somewhat proud when I make Brits uncomfortable by pretending I don't understand their cultural cues.

Coping with big emotions

" *Anna, are you coming here tomorrow to play with me?*'" my four-year-old niece asks on Skype. She's in Finland and me, well, I'm in London and clearly not going to make this play date.

This is one of the many times it feels absolutely unbearable to live abroad and away from my family.

There are things happening back home I will miss, and there are things happening in my life I cannot share with people because of lack of that physical presence. Over the years, missing people has become a nearly normal emotion, something that is so present in my everyday life that I can actually ignore it every now and then and focus my energy on other things.

The truth is, I miss someone *all the time.* Even when all of us experience this same emotion for sure, believe me, it takes a whole new shape when I'm in another country. There are not many things I can do immediately to ease this pain, and it also requires a more active approach to make sure I stay in touch with all these people. What I have done is turned missing into a positive emotion and something I can draw energy from. I'm fortunate to have people I miss dearly and who are making a difference in my life even when they are far away. Today, I respect my roots, family, friends (and distance) on a completely new level, and how well I deal with these emotions is high priority for my wellbeing.

When I look on the other side of the coin, there's a lot of magic when I go back home. The gratitude of being there and spending time with people I care about is something I treasure for a long time, even after the event. I'm more present in those moments, and because there's never enough time, I always invest in making memories, big or small, to take with me when I travel back "*home.*" I still get emotional when I leave Finland (or any other special place), but in a weird way these days, it makes me happy I'm missing someone. It means there's a reason to go back.

If I were to move abroad now, I would most likely tell myself to:

- Be open, positive and curious about everything – the whole idea of moving is to have more fun and adventure in life, right?!

- Have faith things will be ok – they will, but sometimes it might take a while, and make you convinced the world is just messing with you... Patience is a virtue!

- Find friends quickly and buddy up – life is so much more fun together. Get out of the house, go to that fancy event, talk to strangers, do whatever fills your boots.

- Leave your ego at the door and ask for help. Like seriously.

- Enjoy the process! It's hard work but the person who comes out at the other end will blow everyone's mind!

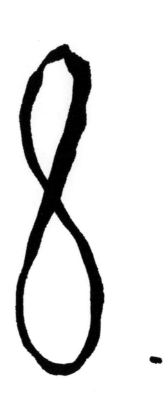

Be and Do Together

Being nice – to myself and others

A few years back I got invited to an occasion where one of my long-term idols was also going to be. To say the least, I was ecstatic and joyous about the opportunity to be in the proximity of this entrepreneur, smart and uber talented woman – to be honest, for a long time I had wanted to be like her!

Much to my disappointment the encounter did not live up to my expectations. To make a long story short, she was not exhibiting the qualities I would expect someone like her to have. There's this particular moment that stood out like a sore thumb: her being rude to the waiter. I thought to myself if you're nice to others but rude to the waiter... she would treat me the same were I the waiter. My opinion of her changed in a blink of an eye.

At the end of the day, the titles, money, cars and all that jazz don't matter one forking bit if the insides are not attractive. I believe what we experience of someone on the outside is the reflection of their deepest self. Behind this there's a mindset about how we show up to others and to the world – and this mindset needs to be trained until the grey matter hurts.

As discussed in the leadership chapter, mastering those internal emotions requires a tremendous amount of never-ending work and accepting oneself is a prerequisite for finding authenticity. Why it is so important we start with ourselves is because we get back exactly what we put out there – aka put out s***, get s*** back. I try to be nice to myself at all times to make things easier in my life. This will help me to show up with my best self – and this is when things get on a roll.

My top tips for upping your niceness game pronto:

- Be nice to people around you – from the barista to the boss. Being nice doesn't cost anything but it can pay you back a hundredfold.

- Cultivate kindness wherever you go. Even better if you smile while you're on it!

- Hold judgement and give praise instead – you'll be surprised how differently people respond.

- Stop complaining and criticizing. The flaws we see in others are often the reflections of our hidden, deepest selves. Keep this in mind when you next open your mouth.

- Be the master of your own brand: how you show up and engage with others shows your true character. People will always remember how you made them feel.

Getting my tribe together

"You are the average of five people around you." When I heard this for the first time, it rocked my world. It is so true that close relationships not only improve the quality of your life significantly, but they also change you as a person. For me it is so important who I let influence myself, my thoughts and my world

You can't select your family (thankfully mine is great!) but you can select your friends – and I want to make sure I have the most amazing humans as friends! When I started contemplating what extraordinary means to me in a friendship, my long-standing BFF emerged as an exemplary case study. We met when we were both at our teens and funnily enough, since then we have rarely lived on the same continent, yet our friendship is so solid not even a hurricane could disturb it.

While our journeys have been very different, it is the gusto and rigor we've done these journeys with that brings us close together in a very intimate way. The reflection points she is able to provide me with, from the other side of the world, mean everything to me, since it comes from a place of experience – she has been where I am. She can relate when I say I miss home; how good I feel after a challenging multi-cultural teleconference meeting is successfully over or how overwhelmed I am over the challenges I'm facing in my new territory. We are similar enough in our values and what we seek to do in our lives. She is my biggest fan. And I am hers. We want to see each other succeed and we will do whatever it takes to support each other on the journey there – heck we want to share the boat! This to me is a remarkable example of a transformational relationship.

When it comes to work, I can honestly say as a consultant I've spent a fair share of my time in the office. Some of the late nights were not as terrible as they might sound, mainly because I got to work with some super smart and talented professionals with both high IQ and EQ. During my consulting career I have experienced first-hand what it means when you have a good team in place: these people have helped me grow and together we have been striving after a shared goal, knowing we would pick each other up should someone fall. For me, knowing I can trust my team is a prerequisite for delivering a high-quality piece of work. My people have opened doors for me to places I could have not gone by myself. And now, even after my corporate door is shut behind me, they're still there for me.

If there's one thing that has made a huge impact on my life and the results I've gotten, it's the coaches and mentors that have partaken in my journey. I'm a strong advocate of coaches to lead the way and show us how it's done with style. While my education in Finland was completely free of charge (some of the many benefits of this amazing country), I have since spent five figures into my own personal development and I am expecting to have spent six figures in the near future. I believe putting my own skin into the game, wearing my grown-up pants and stepping up to the occasion are non-negotiable requirements to achieve results that measure on a completely different scale. Making some sizeable investments into the most precious asset of my life, myself. Let's be honest here: these goals are not just whatever small feats, but I'm talking about the achieve world peace, stop wars, and change the lives of 3 million women types of goals that make your legs weak.

What my mentors and coaches have taught me – sometimes demanded of me – has enabled me to not only make small steps but leaps in my own thinking and life. It's like the most complicated relationship when in one moment they make me the most nervous ever, challenging me to leave my comfort zone and then in the next moment we're patting each other's backs. You gotta love 'em!

Grow from Failure

Failure is feedback

I can tell you that being in New York, late at night, on the street somewhere in Lower East Side, and finding out you have really been screwed with your rental apartment is not something to aspire to. It made me miss my parents. I wanted to sit on the sidewalk and cry like a baby. Actually, I wanted to cry into my empty wallet.

How we handle these moments matters. It can be a character-defying moment when you put yourself back together and decide to move forward. At the very basic level, we only change as a consequence of pleasure or pain, and personally, I've found the latter to be quite the catalyst for me to make necessary changes and to make them right away. I have a very low tolerance for things that make me cringe, and if it's in my control zone, I'm going to do something about it.

When I've been faced with disappointments, I try my best to accept it – and boy, this for me is still so hard! But these things happen, so I let my frustration come out. Then I get serious about it all and try to be brutally honest about why things actually went wrong. Like with that New York pad – that was entirely due to my own stupidity. I made some mental notes to make sure I wouldn't repeat the same thing all over again, because that would be absolute insanity!

Finally, it's time to go at it again! I will try for as long as I need to. Change the process, change the outcome. Personally, I believe no one will say no forever. We can learn from our setbacks, and while we cannot stop obstacles from appearing, we can choose how we handle them. They may make us paralysed for a moment, but if we persevere, we can discover opportunities that have always been waiting for us on the other side. As we get more efficient with this process, we enable ourselves to see beyond failure.

Between failure and success, there is one more try. Other great things to remember (also as a reminder to my tender soul...) are:

- As discussed earlier, the confidence mindset needs training. Keep the faith that things will turn out ok...it might look like the universe is having fun at your expense, but the table will turn, believe me.

- Be sensitive to your feelings when things are not going well – accept all emotions but don't drown into the pool. Keep moving and focus on building the new. Nothing amazing ever came out of resentment last time I checked.

- When shit hits the fan, you're close to the solution. Keep going, sister/brother.

- Call mom and spend an hour crying into the phone. You'll feel better (and she'll be more worried...)

Pain fueling personal growth

Some mistakes are huge and come with a lot of pain. I'm talking about the heart-wrenching type of pain that comes mostly from relationships. Before, I was the girl who ignored this kind of pain, not taking stock and quickly moving on. It's not that I didn't care about others or what was going on, but the fact was, I didn't want to look at my flaws close-up. I guess I have always been challenged by the idea of stepping back and seeing myself without any masks and with complete honesty. I have come to understand how important it is to know exactly where one stands – even if it's a terrible sight – in order to make real progress.

Nearly nine years ago, I was put into a proper test when my long-standing relationship turned upside down nearly overnight. Details aside, it was like a rug had been pulled from underneath me and I was lying on the floor unable to catch my breath. I can tell you I spent many hours lying on several floors and friends sofas before I could put the pieces of my soul back together. I couldn't understand why this had happened to me, nor could I understand what I had done wrong. The pain was so present in each and every moment and I felt like my poor heart was held together by a thin rubber band, about to burst any minute.

Over a freezing cold and snowy Finnish winter slow healing started to take place. I understood retreating back into myself was not only important to get to know the real me, but also an absolute necessity in order to rebuild the new. I embraced all the feelings as raw as they arrived and stayed patient with myself and with how I was feeling. While recognised the deep sadness within me, I felt it was imperative to experience it in all its power and glory, and to accept whatever was arising from my body and from my subconscious mind. Bit by bit, I could feel a new story forming that would ultimately help me to move on in my life.

This was a transformational period in my life, and reflecting on it now, I can see how I grew as a person – and as a woman. I did not shy away from any feelings. I worked on myself, kept close to my family, and reached out to friends for support and help. I knew this was going to pass, and I actually tried hard to live in the present moment, even amidst the pain. As a result, I could feel how my mind was getting stronger. I knew I was worthy, and my capacity to love was still there. I continued to believe in the good in people without wasting my energy on people or things I could not change. Most importantly, I now had absolute certainty I could heal my wounds myself and look after my body, mind and soul with tender-loving care.

So, when that magical spring morning arrived, and my conscious mind was ready to realise that being happy each and every day came down to me and myself only, my life changed in a blink of an eye. I made this one simple decision: to be happy. I allowed this joy to arrive into my soul, letting my heart skip a beat. I smiled as I recognised this familiar feeling...the original Anna was back. I gave her a very warm hug.

I would not change any of my excruciating experiences. Maybe they were even blessings in disguise. I am a firm believer that in the end, I will only regret the chances I didn't take, the relationships I was afraid to have, and the decisions I took too long to make. And you all know how this story ends: my London dream was born as a consequence of these events...and look at me now! Because of everything have done in my life so far, I stand where I stand today

10.

Seek Immersion and Experience Magic

Frequently unloading

The huge travel bug that bit me at a very young age has led me to several interesting situations, including the following;

At the young age of 19, I stood at Newark Airport in New Jersey, US. This was the start of my au pair career, looking after two kids for the period of three months. It's fair to say I felt a bit nervous, mostly because this was my first time in the US, and I had never been away from home for this long... and I had never, ever looked after kids. But hey, what could go wrong?!

At 23, I found myself down under in Australia, at the Sydney Dance Company's lobby, waiting for my turn to audition for Moulin Rouge in Paris (I know it's weird, right...). We had just been through the one-minute choreography, and I could not remember any of the steps. I felt very uncomfortable in fishnets and a tiny bodice. I wanted to escape or at least put some proper clothes on.

At 30, my career took me to Johannesburg, South Africa, where I was working for a local bank as a part of an international consulting assignment. We had enjoyed an amazing weekend at the Kruger National Park. However, now we were required to organise a team to improve the efficiency in this team, and I could feel my negotiation skills were not up to snuff

I'm aware I have been very lucky to be able to roam this world and to feed my never-ending wanderlust. I am also very aware of how privileged my life is (and the lives of many others who live in the West), for I have seen the realities of other people. The experiences I have had and the lessons I have learned while traveling are things that are not taught in schools. These experiences have changed me in unimaginable ways, and they have made me richer in so many ways. Getting out of our usual habitat and getting lost somewhere unfamiliar are quick tools to expand ourselves and our thinking exponentially in a very rapid manner.

I'm aware not many people like traveling solo, but I found this type of travel works for me. Instead of feeling lonely, I carry my books and notebook with me. I create a solid itinerary to hit the best museums and even a yoga class. As it turns out, when I travel alone, I need to make more effort to get in contact with other people – and actually, talking and engaging with strangers can be a thrilling experience! You would be surprised how keen people are to interact if you just keep an open mind. Also, there's something about the ability to press pause and be alone with your thoughts (even if it's forced). This is a superhuman skill in my opinion. In today's world where even the library isn't quiet anymore, these extended pauses in a faraway land might be just what the doctor ordered. You might even get some new ideas!

I have never had any issues whatsoever travelling as a solo female. However, I always make safety a priority and won't take any unnecessary risks. This means taking taxis in the evening, not walking alone anywhere that looks/feels/sounds suspicious, always watching over my food and drinks, etc. I recommend using your common sense and heightened sense of caution, in particular when travelling in less developed countries.

Oh, and what did I get out of those three trips? Well, the New Jersey experience was mind-blowing! The kids behaved (mostly), I trained ballet with the New Jersey Ballet, got into a bar (illegally, but hey)

and went to Manhattan each and every weekend
In Sydney, I didn't get into Moulin Rouge because
apparently while I was very creative with my steps, I
was too fat. (To be fair, those girls are tiny.) Finally, I
fell in love with South Africa, its culture and people.
The work part was tough, but at the end, I had a
happy client and I had seen the big five.

How would I recommend feeding your wanderlust?

- Book that trip now! There's a big world out
  there and things to experience you cannot
  experience watching Netflix. Also, traveling
  today is not as expensive as most people
  assume – for me it's cheaper to be in Bali for
  a month compared to living in London...just
  saying!

- Be brave while abroad – start that
  conversation, go to that bar alone, smile to
  a stranger. What's the worst thing that can
  happen – they smile back?!

- However, don't be stupid. Always pay extra
  attention when traveling, keep your eyes
  open and follow local rules and regulations.

- Get into the local groove – I personally like

to get outside the beaten path and meet real locals. If you get to hear their stories, I promise it will rock your world.

• Have fun, be different, feel the wind in your hair. Life is here and now <3

Experiencing significant personal growth

There's the irregular, shorter travel that I love... and then there's the fully immersive version, the one where you lose yourself and then find yourself again. Where you experience true magic. This type of travel is what my heart lives for. When I'm out of my typical surroundings, there's an alluring scent of a fascinating opportunity for personal growth unfolding right in front of my eyes.

One of these magical journeys was my tango fiesta in the gorgeous city of Buenos Aires in South America in 2017. One of my long-standing dreams was to learn the Argentine tango, and when I was reaching my five-year anniversary in London, I thought to myself now is the time. In my mind's eye, the Argentine tango is the sexy, sultry, somewhat melancholic tango that has been called to resemble love-making in a vertical position. Women can express their goddess elements and the men lead these Venuses to pastures new. I wanted some of that.

So off I went! My plan of attack for the two months was to learn directly from professional dancers, take one-on-one lessons, and basically dance as much as I could, whenever the opportunity would arise. I would let the night turn into morning on the pista of a heated, sweaty milonga. I would wear the most gorgeous, sparkling stilettos and dream in my partner's arms. (I should also say that while my background is in ballet, I'm completely clueless when it comes to social dancing...!). And woah, what a beautiful experience this tango journey ended up being! While learning to dance, I also made some wonderful new connections that will last a lifetime. I learned a little bit of Spanish, explored everything Buenos Aires has to offer and – most importantly – stepped back from my normal routines.

While the dance steps are important, so is the

personal transformation that occurs during these extended periods of travel. When I've focused on something completely different, things have started to happen. My thought process works differently. A new opinion, thought, idea, or skill starts to form, and my brain finally has some time to handle all of it. There's time to focus on the now – sometimes, it's almost like time slows down. There's less noise and less to do while simultaneously there's more focus and more determination. I have made some of my biggest decisions, experienced aha-moments, and found new things about myself while on these travels. Looking into anything deeper and with more detail, whether it be yourself or the world, is where huge potential lies. I keep doing this because this type of travel inspires my life for a very long time.

A word of warning though: I have traveled and experienced some mind-blowing things, and sometimes it's only when I come back home that I can see how much I have changed. For example, as a result of that innocent Buenos Aires tango trip, I made the decision to quit my consulting job. So, travel at your own risk ☺

WHAT'S NEXT?

In April 2018, I closed the door to corporate consulting after being somewhat married to the profession for nearly ten years. While I have always felt my current profession and job is the right one for me, the journey I've done in consulting has made me come closer to the woman I was always destined to be, and this is a step away from my consultant role as I see it.

After coming back from Buenos Aires, I suffered from pneumonia. On top of that, my boss resigned, and January in London is not the most exciting month anyways. Sleeping on my colleague's floor on an air mattress as I was waiting to sign a new lease, some really thought-provoking questions started entering my mind. I was upset and knew I needed to step back to clarify my vision. Our thoughts tend to get cloudy over time, and mine were certainly having a very cloudy season.

I felt like I was standing at a crossroads, needing reinvention. Something was nudging me to continue my journey. I wondered about the questions I might ask myself at the end of my life... I knew I wanted to make a big impact on the world. I wanted to love more and to have a partner to magnify it all, and I wanted to leave something behind that would make people say: "*This Anna the Amazon really made my life so much better!*" At the end of this thinking, I was very aware something would need to radically change to achieve this very different outcome.

Nearly a year has passed since that realisation. I already feel how I have stepped into a more authentic role for me, and I'm really enjoying it all! I'm thrilled to be an entrepreneur and a business owner, and I'm stoked to bring my new business in coaching available to my tribe. In my personal vision, I state: "*I want to support others in exploring and finding their true nature and unlimited potential. ... I seek to give, contribute, inspire and teach where it adds value. I want to lead by example and am equipped to show others the art of possible. My work with individuals, teams and communities not only connects me to these beings, but I am a vehicle that connects people to each other in a beautiful and sustainable way.*"

This is my calling, and I'll do my best in serving it. It's never too late, and for me, round three is just about to start! Please join me on the journey with the Wander Woman Tribe!

TIPS FOR LIVING AND WORKING IN LONDON

About living in London

Oh, London! One of the greatest cities in the world! Below are some key takeaways from my six years in London. Enjoy!

London has about ten million inhabitants, so it is busy over here. Moving about, and commuting takes time, so the right mindset is definitely required. Thankfully, we do have one of the best transportation systems in the world, so tubes, buses, Overground, trains, DLR, taxis and Boris bikes take you anywhere in London. These days, I even cycle... I know, right!

London is expensive. Most people flatshare, and the flats are often on the smaller size. I know the old Victorian buildings are exquisite, but it can get breezy over the winter months. Prepare to spend more across all categories of life, be it accommodation, transportation, food, or services.

Whatever tickles your fancy, we have it! From art, culture, ballet, and opera to football, restaurants, shopping, etc. – London has it all! This is one of the key reasons I moved here, and I have taken full advantage of the cultural entertainment that can be found in this town.

It actually rains less than people think. However, we can have four seasons in one day, so don't trust the view from the window in the morning. Always carry an umbrella and have some common sense with shoes!

The food is amazing, and you will be spoilt for choice, whatever cuisine you might be after. People like to go out to eat, so always make a reservation if it's possible, especially on the weekend. Home delivery works superbly. I get groceries delivered to my front door, and organic, local, vegetarian and vegan are increasingly popular. There's no excuse to not eat healthily in London!

About working in London

London is an amazing city for nearly any type of professional. It is the hot spot for the best talent and expertise for any discipline. This also means there's competition for the best placements.

London is an uber-international and social city. People don't bat an eyelid when they face a foreign accent. Londoners are used to working with a diverse crowd, so don't worry.

The working culture is more informal when compared to Nordic countries for example. You get more involved with the team after work and through other activities, and it's not uncommon to know your colleagues' spouses and kids, too.

The after-work culture is alive and well. While not my cup of tea, Londoners like to enjoy a pint or two after work, basically on any day during the week.

People put in proper hours and the work week can get pretty long. In consulting, it was not rare to tick 80+ hours on the clock, and I've heard of bankers and lawyers who take a sleeping bag to work and sleep under their desk. Add commuting, and 9 to 5 can be a faraway dream.

Everyone is really busy – respect that. Arrive to meetings on time. Prepare for the meeting properly send an agenda and objectives beforehand and study he topic you're going to discuss) so you can make he most of the actual face time. Always follow-up oon after the meeting if you're keen for the person o remember you! LinkedIn works really well here, t least in the professional services industry. With lients I know better, we often text or even use VhatsApp.

Get creative with your working style – be mobile nd ready to be on the go. I pack all my gear in the norning (work + dance/yoga stuff + snacks) and use ong travel times to catch up on email, read my book, sten to a podcast...

While the 3/4g network is sometimes comparable o being in a desert, there's reliable Wi-Fi nearly verywhere. People work from cafes, libraries and otel lobbies. There's a growing number of organised ree-form office space where you can work more or ess 24/7. Maybe you don't even need a pad ☺

We Londoners dine "al desk." Canary Wharf lone welcomes over 100,000 workers daily which leans there's no space for everyone to have a sit-down lunch. According to my own study, the real reason for al desk is that you basically have no time to eat, so you munch your lunch while (inefficiently) filling in your Excel sheet.

London is great for networking and after work events are a norm. Relationship building with clients goes beyond formal meetings, so get your cocktail dress ready.

Life here can get stressful – understand what stresses you out and try to minimise it. For me, the thought of being late (I'm never late!) causes stress, so I always leave (too) early.

TIPS FOR SUCCEEDING IN MANAGEMENT CONSULTING

I got into management consulting about 10 years ago and it's been such a fun profession! I have enjoyed the challenge, variety, and opportunities this profession has provided, and the job has suited my personality very well. I'm an outgoing, ambitious achiever and enjoy being with people.

The skills I've acquired in management consulting are very useful as they translate across different professions, roles, and industries. Consulting attracts some bright individuals (great to learn from), smart clients (great to work with) and a huge opportunity to learn in a way that is fun, engaging, and challenging. Finally, a lot of the skills are useful in life overall: planning, the ability to organise, leadership and interpersonal skills, among others!

Over the years, as I have led a variety of projects and teams, I have come to appreciate certain characteristics in my colleagues, particularly in the junior members of the team. These skills have essentially made my life *easier*. I know these traits are also valued elsewhere, and for me, they really are at the core of a true professional who has the ability to add value wherever she lands.

Here we go...

- Say yes! Who cares if it's not your job; do it anyway. Be the person who doesn't mind getting her hands dirty but is solely focused on getting the job done.

- Constantly add more value than expected. Go beyond that extra mile and always strive to improve.

- Be someone your colleagues can trust– you'll be given more important work in no time.

- Know your stuff and practice x10,000. Prepare for all possible scenarios and practice in front of mirrors, together with your friends and even ask your mom to give you feedback.

- Develop an ability to think on your feet; sometimes answers need to arrive to clients quickly. If you don't know, say you don't know but you shall find out. Be diplomatic.

- Don't get stuck at the first obstacle but be resourceful and use your grey matter. Approach others with solutions, not problems. Shows you can think.

- Simplicity is our friend: people don't remember more than three things. Complexity is the enemy of execution. Keep it simple; this is not rocket science.

- If you're able to wrap things into a story, even better. People love stories.

- Avoid consulting jargon – people don't get it and you want your client to look and feel smart. (Our job as consultants is to make them look good.)

- Always, and I mean always, pay great attention to detail (getting into trouble with a contract is something you don't want to lose your job for).

- Use your common sense. Thinking is good and often underestimated!

- Develop your ability to handle the political, the rational and the emotional. We are all humans working in complex organisations and trying to make it work.

- While it's important to know how to play politics, let the quality of your work speak for itself – at all levels.

- Ask good questions, but think before you ask. No one knows everything, but the quality of the answer is entirely dependent on the quality of the question.

- Think about the outcomes and have flexibility in the process. Know when you can go for it and ask for forgiveness later.

- Listen. As they say, when you talk, you're just repeating what you know already, but when you listen, you have the opportunity to learn.

- Keep your eyes open for learning opportunities. Do things that challenge you and are outside your comfort zone. People who think their job is boring have not exhausted all the opportunities available to them.

- Work with people who are more experienced, think differently than you, and who are keen to share their insights – the payback will be tremendous.

- Be a team player. Be a nice person. Be someone people actually want to work with.

You never know who you might bump into in the future – remember, a junior member of the team might be your future boss!

- Be the leader, no matter your title or rank. Show leadership in all situations and develop your character and personal ethos outside of work, too.

- Show your personality and be the beautiful, unique you! People buy people and they fall in love with personalities.

ADDITIONAL RESOURCES

Self-improvement books (non-fiction):

- Chris Anderson: TED Talks

- Brene Brown: The Gifts of Imperfection: Let Go of Who You Think You're Supposed to Be and Embrace Who You Are

- Dale Carnegie: How to Win Friends and Influence People

- Gary Chapman: The 5 Love Languages

- Jim Collins: Good to Great

- Stephen R. Covey: The 7 Habits of Highly Successful People

- Mason Currey: Daily Rituals

- Mihaly Csikszentmihalyi: Flow. The Classic Work on How to Achieve Happiness.

- Ray Dalio: Principles

- Carol Dweck: Changing The Way You Think to Fulfil Your Potential

- David Eagleman: The Brain – The Story of You
- Tim Ferriss – Tools of Titans; Tribe of Mentors; 4-hour Workweek
- Seth Godin: Tribes
- John Kotter: The Sense of Urgency
- Yuval Noah Harari: Sapiens. A brief history of humankind.
- Cal Newport: Be so good they cannot ignore you
- Daniel H. Pink: To Sell is Human
- Tony Robbins: Awaken the Giant Within; Unshakeable
- Steven Pressfield: The War of Art
- Oskari Saari & Aki Hintsa: The Core: Better life, better performance
- Jen Sincero: You are a badass at making money
- Eckhart Tolle: The Power of Now
- Cleo Wade: Heart Talk – Poetic Wisdom for Better Life

eisure read books (both non-fiction and fiction):

- Marina Abramovic: Walk Through Walls
- Atticus: Love Her Wild
- Charles Bukowski: Factotum
- Viktor Frankl: Man's Search for a Meaning
- Herman Hesse: Siddharta
- Siri Hustvedt: What I Loved
- Grace Jones: I'll Never Write My Memoir
- Phil Knight: Shoe Dog
- Milan Kundera: The Unbearable Lightness of Being
- Sylvia Plath: The Bell Jar
- Ralf Potts: Vagabonding
- Patti Smith: M Train

Inspirational podcasts

- How I Built This with Guy Raz
- Impact Theory with Tom Bilyeu
- Oprah's SuperSoul Conversations
- School of Greatness with Lewis Howes
- The Knowledge Project with Shane Parrish
- The Tim Ferriss Show
- The Tony Robbins Podcast

REMEMBER TO DISCOVER YOUR MAGIC!

Wow, you made it all the way to the end ☺ In case you've forgotten, here's a kind reminder of the gift I want to give to you... How would your own dream-lining plan sound like? Go to my website and download yours – your secret address is:

www.annakuusela.com/youarethebest

Where to find the Tribe and me online...

- Go to annakuusela.com or wanderwomantribe. com – a hub for great content, inspiration and an opportunity to get down to business with me. Don't forget to subscribe to my newsletter!

- On social media Instagram @ wanderwomantribe, my personal handle @ msannaquuu or Facebook @ annawanderwoman. Please use hashtag #wanderwomantribe across all social media platforms so I can see you!

- Send me love letters at anna@annakuusela. com and I will write ya back!

Looking forward to welcoming you to the Tribe!

Printed in Poland
by Amazon Fulfillment
Poland Sp. z o.o., Wrocła